STICKY

STICKY

Andy Croft

FlambardPress

First published in Great Britain in 2009 by Flambard Press
16 Black Swan Court, 69 Westgate Road, Newcastle upon Tyne NE1 1SG
www.flambardpress.co.uk

Typeset by BookType
Cover Design by Gainford Design Associates
Printed in Great Britain by Athenaeum Press, Gateshead

Front Cover Photograph by Richard Jarvis

A CIP catalogue record for this book
is available from the British Library.

ISBN: 978-1-906601-05-8

Flambard Press wishes to thank Arts Council England
for its financial support.

Flambard Press is a member of Inpress.

The paper used for this book is FSC accredited.

for Jean Croft

and in memory of Geoff Croft, 1930–2004

Acknowledgements

Some of these poems were first published in *Acumen*, *Hard Times* (Berlin), *The Interpreter's House*, *The London Magazine*, *Modern Poetry in Translation*, *The Morning Star*, *The Northern Echo*, *Penniless Press*, *PN Review*, *Poems about Southwell* and *Red Pepper*; in Andy Croft (ed.), *Holme and Away* (Bar None Books, 2004), Claire Malcolm (ed.), *Magnetic North* (New Writing North, 2006), Bob Beagrie and Andy Willoughby (eds), *The Wilds* (Ek Zuban, 2007), Andy Croft (ed.), *Speaking English* (Five Leaves, 2007), W.N. Herbert (ed.), *A Balkan Exchange* (Arc, 2007) and John Rety (ed.), *Well Versed* (Hearing Eye, 2009).

The poems in Part III were commissioned by the South Bank Centre, London, for Poetry International 2006 to mark the fiftieth anniversary of the death of Bertolt Brecht. The poems in Part V were written while working as writer-in-residence at HMP Holme House in Stockton-on-Tees from 2000–03. The poems in Part VI were commissioned by the Southwell Poetry Festival in 2006. 'A Theory of Devolution' was originally commissioned by BBC North East and broadcast on BBC2's *The Politics Show* in 2004. 'Live from Revolution Square, Mudfogistan' was commissioned by BBC Radio Cleveland and written during election night, 2005. 'Human Estate' was commissioned by Arts UK; parts of the poem appear on road-signs designed by the sculptor Andrew Burton in the new housing estate on Dixon's Bank, Middlesbrough.

The author would like to acknowledge the financial support of a New Writing North Time to Write Award and of the Cultural Sector Development Initiative.

Contents

I
Sticky   10

II
The Baron Munchausen Bar, Sofia   16
Kartichka   19
Rotunda   20
Martenitsa   21
There Was a Spirit in Europe   22

III
An Offer You Can't Refuse   26
Reading Brecht in the Bath   28
Miami Song   29
Echt   30
Supply and Demand   34
In the Brecht Museum   36

IV
Jet-Lag in Barabashkagorod   38
A Russian Diary   41
Idiot Snow   48
Idiot Bag   49
Lesson   50

V
The Ballad of Writing Gaol   52
Black and Blue   57
Villain-elle   58
Honest   59
How Do You Spell Heroin?   60
Form   61
Team Strip   62
Zoology   63
Away!   64

VI

Either or Eyether	66
Faith: Southwell Minster	68
Hope: Southwell Races	69
Charity: Southwell Workhouse	70
Little Green Men	71

VII

A Question of History	74
A Theory of Devolution	75
Dirty Work in Mudfog	79
Live From Revolution Square, Mudfogistan	81
Human Estate	82
Red Ellen	84
This Is Not a Poem	85

VIII

Too Much	88
By Heart	89
Whatever	90
Go!	91
Checkpoint Charlie	92
Foggiest	93
They Think It's All Over	94
Clerihew and Cry	97
Not So	99

IX

Letter to Randall Swingler Part III	102

I

Sticky

'By our efforts, we have lit a fire . . . a fire in the minds of men. It warms those who feel its power, it burns those who fight its progress, and one day this untamed fire of freedom will reach the darkest corners of our world.'
George W. Bush

for Adrian Mitchell at 75

One sticky summer afternoon
  Three boys were playing near a wood;
They made a swing, played hide-and-seek,
  And ran around as children should.
Then, gathering some twigs and sticks
  They built a little cairn until
They only needed bigger sticks
  To light a fire, as children will.

Beneath the ancient family tree
  The sticks were watching in alarm,
'What's going on?' Simplistick asked,
  Said Idealistick, 'just stay calm.'
'I don't like this one little bit,'
  Said Pessimistick; 'I suggest,'
Beamed Optimistick, 'we will find
  It's bound to turn out for the best.'

'No doubt they'll put me on the top,
  Where I belong,' Bombastick boomed,
'It doesn't matter anyway,'
  Wailed Fatalistick, 'we're all doomed.'
Unrealistick then piped up,
  'They're going to build a dinosaur!'
'Of course, they are,' Sarcastick said,
  'That's what they've got those matches for.'

'It's obvious,' Majestick said,
    'That I'm the stick that they require.'
Artistick said, 'I do so hope
    We're going to make a lovely fire.'
'I'd like to know,' Statistick mused,
    'How many sticks they're going to need.'
Scholastick looked up from his book,
    'Look can't you see I'm trying to read?'

'What's going on?' Simplistick asked,
    'I'm not so sure,' Agnostick sighed,
'I wish I knew – it's hard to say –
    It all depends – I can't decide.'
Iconoclastick threw some stones,
    Enthusiastick tried to dance,
Acoustick strummed, Monastick hummed,
    While Mystick fell into a trance.

When all the sticks were gathered up
    They lay in one enormous heap,
'We've had it,' Fatalistick groaned.
    Somnambulistick fell asleep.
Said Masochistick 'Will it hurt?'
    'I'm sure it will,' Sadistick hissed,
'How awful,' Altruistick sniffed,
    Domestick snarled and clenched his fist.

The boys then stuffed the bonfire's base
    With piles of leaves and bits of paper,
They passed a box of matches round,
    And tried to light the home-made taper.
Just then the wind began to blow,
    The matches flickered in the breeze,
Said Nationalistick with a snort,
    'Those matches aren't from *British* trees.'

Eventually the fire was lit,
    The little flames grew hotter, higher,
'How beautiful!' Artistick said,
    And fell into the glowing fire.
The flames began to lick the sticks,
    'That tickles!' Masochistick yelped,
'I bet it does,' Sadistick grinned,
    Realistick shrugged, 'It can't be helped.'

'I do so hope I look my best,'
    Said Narcissistick with a smile,
'If I am going up in flames
    At least I'm going to go in style.'
'What's going on?' Simplistick asked,
    Fantastick said, 'It's just a joke.'
'It's wonderful!' Ecstatick gasped,
    And vanished in a puff of smoke.

Ecclesiastick said a prayer,
    Gymnastick balanced on her head,
'Let's face it,' Fatalistick shrugged,
    'It's obvious we'll soon be dead.'
'I must protest,' Bombastick boomed,
    'I'm far too valuable to die!'
'I knew it,' Pessimistick groaned.
    Nihilistick laughed, 'The End is Nigh!'

Then Communistick raised his voice,
    'We can't just branch out on our own,
We must resist – all sticks unite,
    Together stronger than alone!'
'I'm not a stick!' Majestick barked,
    'I'm more a branch – or else a bough,'
'A Special Branch!' Sarcastick smirked,
    'It's time you twigged you're firewood now.'

Said Egotistick, 'I don't care
  What happens to the rest of you,
I've packed my trunk, I'm outta here –'
  Ballistick broke him clean in two.
'I saw that!' Voyeuristick said,
  'So what?' Antagnonistick snapped.
Elastick jumped on Plastick's head,
  Evangelistick loudly clapped.

'What's going on?' Simplistick asked,
  Anachronistick swore an oath,
Surrealistick yelled, 'A fish!'
  Antagonistick punched them both.
And so the sticks began to fight.
  As they were eaten by the fire,
And one by one the silly sticks
  Became each other's funeral pyre.

The moral of this sticky story
  Of sticks who were too proud to bend,
Is we must learn to stick together
  Or else we'll meet a sticky end.
Although the earth is hotting up
  We can't agree on what to do,
So stick around and ask yourself,
  What kind of silly stick are you?

II

'And after that, Vulgaria became a free country and all the children laughed and played in the sunshine, and they were very, very happy. And Chitty flew high over the mountains back to England, everyone safe and sound, and . . .'

Caractacus Potts in the film *Chitty Chitty Bang Bang*

The Baron Munchausen Bar, Sofia

'We drink, we sing with recklessness,
We snarl against the tyrant foe,
The taverns are too small for us,
"To the mountains we shall go."'
       Hristo Botev

for Bill Herbert

You follow the yellow-brick road through the snow,
Past the topless young girls on the highway,
Through Horrible Valley and Terrible Pass
Till at last you will come to a doorway.

It's tucked between Schweik's and Flanagan's Bar,
Down a side-street of uneven cobbles,
But once you're inside you know you're with friends
Who will help you forget all your troubles.

Inside it's so crowded and smoky and dark
That you can't tell one hand from the other;
Here a Yes means a No and a No means a Yes,
And the neighbouring sexes mean either.

You hang up your hang-ups just inside the door
In exchange for a small token gesture,
Sly Peter will offer to buy you a beer
And ask you to drink to the future.

And after a while you can see that it's full
Of artists in shades and black leather,
Like talking heads chained in the inferno-dark
They talk of new sins and old lovers.

Here the bar-maids are lovely as Catherine the Great,
And the beer tastes as cold as the Iskar;
On TV the football is never nil-nil,
And the Hristos are wrapping up Moskva.

And the peppers are red as CSKA shirts,
And the vegetable soup is near solid
With the flesh of the Chopski, that gentlest of tribes,
Who taught us all how to make salad.

Here the regulars vote for a fairy-tale king,
Who it's rumoured supports Barcelona,
He doesn't like children but comes in to drink
With the tough-looking boys in the corner.

Each night if you want you can drink the bar dry
As long as the Baron has credit,
Though the menu's as large as the Vitosha hills,
The bill is so small you can't read it.

If ever you leave here (and some never do)
You will find that the snow is still falling,
In Battenberg Square they've forgotten the date,
And the frozen-tongued bells have stopped pealing;

And the skate-boarders spin round the partisan dead
In the gardens on Boulevard Levski,
And the tomb of Dimitrov's been swapped overnight
For an oversize bottle of whisky;

And the past is as clean as the streets under snow,
And everyone's tired and sleepy,
And the future's as bright as the man in the moon,
And freedom makes everyone happy;

And the statues outside are stiff with the cold,
And the girls by the road are still topless;
And the children of beggars are sleeping outside,
And the cold constellations are helpless.

The Baron untethers one half of his horse
Which he tied to an Orthodox steeple,
And wishes you all a merry good night
As he flies off to Constantinople.

Some say he's a con-man, some say he's for real,
Some say that the Baron's in earnest,
But don't take my word for it, go there yourself –
You'll never believe it all. Honest.

Kartichka

Just round the corner from the new hotel
That someone says was built by Russian mafia,
A kind of multi-alphabet dysgraphia
Now flourishes on tree-lined walls which spell
'Red Madness!', 'Lokomotib', 'HE HO HATO',
'bHC', 'Cockney Sparrers Oi! Oi! Oi!',
'CCCP', 'CSKA', 'Destroy!'

Town-planners and utopians since Plato
Have found their well-drawn plans a palimpsest
Through which the scrawl of Babel-tongued graffiti
Can still be read – part threat and part entreaty –
Return of the repressed, in lines addressed
From those who aren't supposed to write at all
To those who've read the writing on the wall.

Rotunda

The woman lights another tapered prayer,
  Whose weeping wax now gutters in the gloom,
  A ritual task which only can illume
A world of superstition and despair.
  Above us, in the bright empyrean blue,
The frieze of flaky prophets on the ceiling
Is laced with holes, as if the heavens were peeling
  To let the pagan night beneath show through.

Behind each fading fresco lies the next,
  Precise as tree-rings, measuring the ages
Of human hope and terror, like a text
  Still legible beneath the parchment pages'
Faint palimpsest. As if such monkish art
Could ever warm this heartless world's cold heart.

Martenitsa

Long, long ago, there was a king
   Who put his foes to flight,
And the victory colours of the spring
   Were bannered red and white.

And the colour of blood is red,
   And white are the snows that fall,
And despite the blood that kings have shed
   The spring belongs to all.

And the victory march of the sun will thaw
   The blood that stains the snow
And hope will spring in the earth once more
   And the red roses grow.

There Was a Spirit in Europe

'When I died at Marathon, I saw this only:
By my head the fennel was growing, slowly.'
Frank Thompson, 1941

'After the firing squad, the worms.'
Nikola Vaptsarov, 1942

Litakovo. The garlic breath of spring
   Begins to thaw the feet of these old hills,
Warm welcome for returning cranes who'll bring
   The luck that resurrects what winter kills.

The frozen fields below begin to stir
   From heavy dreams of snow. The flowers keep
Their vigil for Persephone. The year
   Turns over slowly, after months of sleep.

Cold-fingered Boreas, foundation-king
   Of these cold hills, once wrestled with the sun
To prove that he was stronger than the spring,
   Half froze the world to stone, and almost won.

Two hours and several centuries ago
   We left Sofia's beggared streets behind,
Through silent fields still scorched by months of snow,
   Up hair-pin mountain roads. We crash and grind

Between the Iskar Gorge's narrow walls,
   The thin-ribbed valley sides, the railway line,
Slow monasteries and urgent waterfalls,
   Steep, limestone-dazzle ridges furred with pine.

Prokopnik. Here, May 1944,
   The Second Sofia (Partisan) Brigade
Passed into History, legend, silence, war.
   The place they crossed the river's now decayed

Into a railway stop of weeds and rust
    Beneath an iron mountain made of slag,
Where snow falls grey with coal-breath dirt and dust.
    Prometheus upon his midnight crag.

This is a bleak and plundered place, a true
    Memorial to the young man with a pipe
Depicted on the platform, after who
    The station's named in carved Cyrillic type:

Frank Thompson, British Major, SOE,
    A Wykhamist, a linguist, poet and Red,
A scion of the English bourgeoisie
    Who found in Aeschylus the road that led

Him here to try to set the world ablaze,
    To prove the new was stronger than the old
And almost won; heroic, springtime days,
    Defeated by the armies of the cold.

Across the other side they lost their way,
    As we do now, through villages of cow
And breeze-block, where half-naked infants play
    And Boreas's children pull the plough,

Where women still leave apples for the dead,
    Inter red-pepper-phallused dolls to bring
The rain, and wear the martenitza thread
    To bind the Easter rituals of spring.

Eleshnitsa (Easter Monday). Here
    Where young men pitch-fork straw upon their backs,
They tortured Thompson. Roads that seem so clear
    On maps turn out to be just snow-lined tracks

That disappear into the hills around
    Litakovo, to which the Fascists brought
The captured partisans, this barrow mound
    Among the trees they call the Turkish Fort.

Five common graves of cracked and lichened stone,
   Is all that's left to show where they were shot,
A green memorial, wild and overgrown
   For heroes whom the winter world's forgot.

Their chiselled names now filigreed with moss,
   The five-point star's an ivy-fingered hand
Reproaching the cold future with the loss
   Of what we are ashamed to understand.

Though better known memorials than these
   Have been knocked down by winter's wolfish tread,
Obscurity's preserved, among the trees,
   The short and simple annals of the dead

Who died for truths that no-one now believes,
   Whose posthumous denunciations lie
Upon this woodland grave like fallen leaves –
   First national hero, then a British spy,

Now Soviet agent. Winter's cold estate
   Requires a hard forgetting. So the truth
They knew at Marathon, the Scaean Gate,
   Becomes a frozen elegy for youth.

The beech's opening bud's a falling leaf,
   Tomorrow is as cold as yesterday,
The seeds of Change have shrunk to the belief
   That nothing lasts and all things must decay;

The North Wind blows the petals from the rose,
   The winter wolf destroys the spring-born lamb,
The cow-slip meadow's crushed beneath the snows,
   The child is sacrificed and not the ram;

The ploughed field disinters the buried god,
   The sharpened sickle cuts the harvest wheat,
The prisoner has to face the firing-squad,
   And victory's just a name we give defeat.

III

'When the clock strikes, half past six, babe,
It's time to head for golden light,
It's a good time, for the great taste,
At McDonald's, it's Mac tonight!'

Advert

An Offer You Can't Refuse

*'If sharks ruled the world they would teach the little fish
that it is a great honour to swim into the mouth of a shark.'*
Brecht

for Mike and Anna Wilson

As the actress takes the curtain
 They are cheering in the stalls,
Mack the Knife is out of town, dear,
 Though his name's sprayed on the walls.

O the shark has pretty teeth, dear,
 And he shows them pearly white,
On the east side of this town, dear,
 You can walk home safe at night.

Here the shark is just a story,
 Some old song about some teeth,
Though there's some who think that freedom's
 Just a name for old Macheath.

On the radio, Sunday morning,
 Frank Sinatra swings this town;
You had better watch your back, dear,
 When the walls start tumbling down.

Now the banks are full of money
 And the streets are full of life;
Who's that sneaking round the corner –
 Is that someone Mack the Knife?

All the ladies love a blade, dear,
 And the whole world loves a knave,
But he'll leave you lying bleeding
 And he'll put you in your grave.

You are free to spend your savings
   On expensive merchandise,
And you're free to walk the streets, dear –
   Every freedom has its price.

When the shark bites with his teeth, dear,
   Scarlet billows start to spread,
On the streets young men are shouting,
   Foreign students turn up dead.

Now the knives are coming out, dear,
   And the sharp suits cut like glass,
And there's beggars in the subways
   On the razor edge of class.

Unemployment keeps on rising,
   While the dole keeps going down –
Oh, the line forms on the right, dear,
   Now that Mackie, good old Mackie,
   Now that Mackie is back in town.

Reading Brecht in the Bath

in memoriam John Willett

It is pleasant to relax in a long bath,
Immersed in a good book.
As you wash away the dust of the day,
The flesh sinks beneath the water
And the mind swims free.

In this amphibious, naked place
Everything floats to the drowsy surface.
Only the truth sinks to the bottom.

The book in your hands
Is weighing you down.
You are out of your depth.
You take in water, fish, salt.
The dead swim past you, waving.
But you go on reading.

This is the poetry of drowning,
Useful as stones in a fisherman's pockets.

Your wrists ache, the water's cold,
The page grows damp, your hands grow old,
And you know it is time to bail out.
Still you go on reading.
If you can't swim, there's no point struggling.

Reading Brecht in the bath:
The simple thing
Which is so hard to do.

You do not relax,
But you will not fall asleep.

Miami Song

'Cuba sera pronto libre.'
    George W. Bush

There's a place down south that I'd like you to see,
Where the rum and the coke and the women were free,
You could fish for sharks,
You could dance all night,
And the senoritas knew
How to treat a man right –
O down-town Havana was the place to be,
When the rum and the coke and the women were free.

There's a place down south where I'd like to go,
Where the rum and the women they used to flow,
You could scuba down in Cuba,
Smoke the best cigars –
You could drive along the coast
In 'fifties cars,
O the bars of old Havana were the place to be
When the rum and the coke and the women were free.

There's a place down south that I'd like to visit,
Where the rum and the women were quite exquisite,
You could play the tables,
You could roll some dice,
You could buy a girl a drink
And get your shoes shined nice,
O the brothels of Havana were the place to be,
When the rum and the coke and the women were free.

There's a place down south that I'd like to explore
When the rum and the women are free once more,
We'll grab some ass
And some real estate,
We'll piss on Castro's grave
In the fifty-first state.
So drink up, old buddy, the beers are all on me,
And we're gonna keep drinking till Cuba is free.

Echt

*'He spoke just as he wrote, in a completely direct manner . . .
and using the wonderful, hard, compact, tight-packed
language peculiar to him. We used to call it laughingly a
mixture of Bavarian, Latin, Chinese and Brechtish.'*
    Vladimir Pozner

for Gordon Hodgeon

O don't we love a half-centenary!
Just fifty years of being dead
Entitles you to the machinery
Of 'classic status', though it's said
Outstanding poets get anniversaries
Just so that all their old adversaries
Can settle some outstanding scores
While joining in the world's applause.
There's bound to be more revelations –
The kind that sells so well these days –
Of lies and spies and stolen plays,
The sex-for-textual relations –
There's even poets so brass-necked
To think that they can write in *Brecht*!

It seemed like such a cool commission,
Not one I thought I should decline,
A chance to honour a tradition
I've always thought as being mine.
But now I fear it was imprudent
And I have proved a hopeless student;
My rusty Latin GCEs
Less helpful than my non-Chinese –
It's not surprising that I fluffed it.
Some words appear to make no sense
Unless they're in the future tense.
Although it's not long since he snuffed it,
How difficult, in retrospect,
It is to try to write in *Brecht*.

For those of us who *were* born later,
It's hard to learn the *Brechtish* tongue,
Sometimes the very best translator
Can get those *Ossi* rhythms wrong.
The problem's not just poor technique, as
There are not many native speakers
Still left who are equipped to teach
The plain, undecorated speech
That once was heard in Mahagonny.
Nobody these days wants to speak
In Esperanto, Ancient Greek
Or any lingo down the Swanee –
In short, you really can't expect
Contemporary poets to talk in *Brecht*.

The issue here is partly local;
In England there is not much worse
Than sounding like some earnest yokel
Who tries to write 'committed' verse.
These days we like our poets classy,
Ironic, risky, edgy, *sassy*,
Experimental, wired and cool –
The sort that kids will read in school.
A poem that's worthy and/or serious
Won't get you laughs when you're on stage
Or win you prizes on the page;
We think that verse should be mysterious,
Ambivalent and circumspect.
No wonder we can't write in *Brecht*!

And anyway, it's *so* out-moded
When words like 'Class' are obsolete
(Although we are still incommoded
By beggars sleeping in the street);
We don't believe the world needs changing,
But just a little rearranging.
In other words, we've had enough
Of all that stern and dreary stuff
About the poor – it's so last season
And so Old Labour – we've moved on.
And now the world's one hope is gone.
If you've got Jesus, who needs reason?
It's not surprising we neglect
The task of understanding *Brecht*.

And he thought *his* time on the planet
Was spent in darkness and despair!
The bloodstained butchers who then ran it
Were even worse than Blush and Bair,
So please don't think me too importunate
If I suggest that they were fortunate
Who did not live to see this flood
Of pious lies and oil and blood
(What's *Brechtish* for imperial slaughter?)
They knew the flood would one day end,
A certainty we can't pretend
As we slide further underwater.
I think these tides will rise unchecked
Unless we start to learn some *Brecht*.

Though English is the *lingua franca*
Of empire, terror, lies and war,
First language of the merchant banker,
The second language of the poor.
This *Brechtish* has a different glamour –
No passive mood, a simple grammar,
The hammered coinage of the real,
The music of the commonweal
That's understood by those who own it.
One day, perhaps, we'll learn to teach
Ourselves a fully human speech;
But till we find that we've out-grown it,
A word like *verfremdungseffekt*
Sounds better when it's said in *Brecht* . . .

Supply and Demand

'I've no idea what a man is,
I only know his price.'
Brecht

Oil is sold to the highest bidder
And everybody must have oil,
If we gain control of the oil-fields
We can set the price of a barrel.
Then everyone must pay for oil with dollars
While we can have cheap petrol for our cars.
But what is oil, actually?
> If you think we don't know what oil is,
> This is our standard riposte:
> Of course we know what oil is,
> Only we don't know its cost.

Wars are won by the highest bidder
And no-one can afford to lose,
If we control the market in death
We can set the price of defeat.
Then everyone must pay for our victory parade
While we share out the spoils.
But what is war, actually?
> If you think we don't know what war is,
> This is our standard riposte:
> Of course we know what war is,
> Only we don't know its cost.

Freedom goes to the highest bidder
And everybody wants to be free,
If we gain control of the language
We can set the price of happiness.
Then everyone must learn to pay for freedom
And we are free to do just as we please.
But what is freedom, actually?
    If you think we don't know what freedom is,
    This is our standard riposte:
    Of course we know what freedom is,
    Only we don't know its cost.

The earth belongs to the highest bidder
And everybody must pay the earth,
If we gain control of the whole world
We can set the price of everything.
Then everyone must learn to live off dirt
While we enjoy the fruits of the earth.
But what is earth, actually?
    Do we know, do you know,
    What this thing is called earth?
    Of course we know what the earth is,
    Only we don't know its worth.

In the Brecht Museum

for Karen Leader

Look over there – it's that famous flat cap,
And here are the glasses, a pair of old shoes,

This must be the chair where he worked on those elegies,
These are some paperbacks he never read,

And this is the bed where he suffered the heart-attack,
Here is the time-piece that stopped when he died,

The table is set as though friends are invited,
The bottle is corked and the food is still hot,

In the desk is a poem he never got round to,
That list of suggestions that nobody followed,

And there on the mantelpiece, still in the ashtray,
A half-smoked cigar, the tobacco still burning,

And here by the fire is an unfinished argument,
These are the masks that he liked to put on,

On the wall by the door is a gesture of loyalty,
Here in a drawer is the private despair,

And here is the patience and there is the certainty,
These are the hopes and the unspoken doubts.

Outside the old garden is frozen in moonlight,
In a country that doesn't exist any more,

And over the border's a world that's still waiting
For the sun to come up and the future begin.

IV

'I knew of a man who believed in a land of righteousness. He said: "Somewhere on this earth there must be a righteous land – and wonderful people live there – good people! They respect each other, help each other, and everything is peaceful and good!" . . . And then to this place – in Siberia, by the way – there came a convict – a learned man with books and maps – yes, a learned man who knew all sorts of things – and the other man said to him: "Do me a favour – show me where is the land of righteousness and how I can get there." At once the learned man opened his books, spread out his maps, and looked and looked and he said – no – he couldn't find this land anywhere . . . everything was correct – all the lands on earth were marked – but not this land of righteousness. The man wouldn't believe it . . . "It must exist," he said, "look carefully. Otherwise," he says, "your books and maps are of no use if there's no land of righteousness."'

Maxim Gorky, *The Lower Depths*

Jet-Lag in Barabashkagorod

As the poem comes into land I can feel myself
Slipping beneath the sleepy waves
Of the obsidian sea thousands of feet below us.
A voice coughs like a saw through the ice
In the middle of the lake.
Or is it a fly I can hear in my ear
Buzzing zhh little baby
As it crawls across the page
Like a line of rude starfish
On the bottom of the obscene river?

I awake some time later
In a city of mini-skirts and ice-creams,
Illuminated by bright scientific thoughts.
'Welcome to Space Station Novosibirsk,
First city on the moon, capital of virtual Sibir.'
I order a beer in the bar of the Cyber Hotel,
Designed by five Microsoft engineers
As a 1970s Intourist-retro theme-park,
Where the girls in leather read *Gary Potter*
The voices in the walls
Don't like Tolkein
And Tanya is waiting for her meal to arrive.

Outside, clouds pink as a suitcase
Spin like Tasmanian devils
Dissolving in a god's period.
After a couple more beers
I pick up a Siber-realist newspaper
Where the alphabet is reversed
And the world is turned upside down.
On the front page they are taking samovars to Tuva,
On the sports page, Pushkin has signed for Chelski.
And Tanya is still waiting for her meal to arrive.

I fall asleep watching TV in the bar
As Angelica Houston turns Ivan into a reindeer,
His eye-brows going up and down
Like a bride's nightie.
At the birthday-cake railway station
Bright as icing-sugar snow in Prostokvashino,
The trains arrive from the East before they have left,
Uncle Fyodor never grows up
And Elena laughs at my terrible accent.
And when I awake, I have turned into a snake
And Tanya is still waiting for her meal to arrive.

Once upon a time
I pick up a tiny book about Troy,
Made of rough paper roughly torn
From a *Rough Guide* to toilets.
And I fall asleep reading about a land
Where once upon a time
The mullet-king's daughter
Was loved by a cheese with a male character.
By now, Tanya has not eaten for a week.

The Frenchwoman pulls off her moustache
In the parish of Paris
And orders a macho nacho
Saying, 'Is that a balalaika in your pocket
Or are you just pleased to see me?'
The voice in the wall is still there,
Saying, 'I want to die.'
And the miller tells his tale,
And Tanya, still waiting for her food,
Turns a whiter shade of pale.

Later, inside Barbie Yagar's house
There is a line of broken Putin dolls on the floor
Like eggs containing two nations.
Dima the driver throws his porridge at the wall.
Meanwhile, the man from Sparks
Sings another verse of *Moscow Nights*
And the man from Marx
Flaps like Batman in the square,
And Tanya announces she is going to shoot herself.

By now the poem is beginning to take in water,
So Elena decides to drive the bus to the airport,
Her delicate wrists twisting the wheel in an obstacle race
Over the holes in the road as wide as the Ob.
But we are obliged to stop
By a line of cross animals slowing:
Chickens in tights, ants in cream,
Jousting cats and vampire bats,
A kvacking frog, Dil the salty dog,
Matroskin the cat, striped like a sailor,
And Ermintrude, perched on the shoulder
Of a Siberian tiger from the Taiga.
And as I sink for the last time beneath the waves of oblivion
I can still hear the voice crying in the dark,
'Where is Caroline? Who is David Beckham?
Where is Comrade Laughter? Who is Victor?'

A Russian Diary

'We've all received an education
In something, somehow, have we not?'
     Pushkin

for Andrei, Elena, Ivan, Lika and Tanya

Newcastle airport, early morning,
A sleepy flight to Amsterdam
Then on to Moscow where, still yawning,
We hit the all-day traffic jam,
And inch our way towards the city
Through traffic lights run by committee,
Past billboards in Cyrillic code,
T-34s beside the road,
Past fast-food outlets selling pizza,
Vast scaffold-building sites that rise
Like Tatlin's tower towards the skies,
Until we reach our *gostinitsa*.
So many miles at such a crawl,
It hardly seems we've moved at all.

The morning's spent on tourist duty –
The bright red toy-town Kremlin walls,
The monuments to Work and Beauty
In Moscow's stunning Metro halls,
The Lenin hats, the sunlit dazzle
Of onion domes on weird St Basil,
Old beggar-women squat as trolls,
Like rows of cheap *matryoshka* dolls.
And then the flight to Tolmachova,
A bumpy ride through violent skies;
Our lives spin past before our eyes
So when at last the journey's over
We head straight for some Russian beer
To toast the fact we're in Sibir.

Our first glad morning in Siberia!
The sky is such a brilliant blue
That everyone is feeling cheerier.
First thing today we're off to view
A writing-class taught by Yevgeny
On Sundays mornings for the many
Young writers who must learn to take
Their critics with a piece of cake.
Jet-lag kicks in; our eyes start closing;
We wake-up in the opera-bar
With beer and crisps and caviar.
If this lot does not get us dozing
Then *Iolanthe* surely will.
On TV Spartak win 6-0.

Gymnasia 1, our first school-visit:
The school of which all teachers dream,
The kids' behaviour is exquisite
(No problem here with self-esteem!)
These children are so keen and eager,
Their English better than the meagre
And blunt expression we expect
In schools back home. We can't connect.
Meanwhile, alas, it seems Elena
Finds my poor Russian quite unkempt,
My every mispronounced attempt
To speak it seems to entertain her.
A bitter cup from which to sup.
At least it serves to shut me up.

The frozen morning's bright and shiny,
As snowbound as an unread text;
The Children's Book Museum is tiny
As all its little users. Next
We give the hottest poetry reading
In Russia – no, but that's misleading –
In History! We are so hot
Our sweaty poems begin to blot
Upon the page. Between the speeches,
The stories, poems and epic toasts
The melting audience slowly roasts.
Today's experience clearly teaches
The rule that writers everywhere
Will always generate hot air.

Through silver miles of slender birches
Like naked women in the snow,
To persevere with our researches
In Akademgorodok. So:
Gymnasium 6, nicknamed the 'Ermine',
Whose pupils are, we soon determine,
So educated and so bright
They do not think that they can write!
In perfect English, if old-fashioned,
'We are not Pushkin!' they protest,
As if one poet is only blessed
And creativity is rationed
And art is someone else's job,
Like fishing through the ice-bound Ob.

We cancel our 7.30 meeting,
A consequence of too much wine,
Too many speeches, too much eating,
(We're still inquorate well past nine).
More visits – first a private college
Where creativity and knowledge
Are mixed like eggs and left to set
(Two nations in one omelette
Require new kinds of table manners).
It's Lenin's birthday; in the square
Old comrades huddle in despair
Beneath their hopeless, ragged banners;
'Sad fucks,' says Andrei with a stare,
As if this means he doesn't care.

Our Tanya steps out like a model,
Siberian dress-codes left behind.
For spouting (off mike) racist twaddle
Ron Atkinson has just resigned.
We're at the British Council, reading,
But truth to tell, we're not succeeding;
Although the audience is polite
We have not set the place alight.
Which English version of the Bible
Do we prefer? What do you think
Of noble poets? (We need a drink!)
Would you describe your poets as tribal?
Which Pushkin poem's the most sublime?
Why don't you English poets rhyme?

Our fellow-travellers leave this morning
And now they've gone we've got the blues,
To purge the homesick feelings dawning
We're taken on a river cruise.
After another massive dinner
That doesn't leave us any thinner;
Eventually we disembark
Down river from 'Not Boring Park'.
Tonight it's Serbian Chumbawumba –
They play a wild, sad Balkan-punk
And seem to get more mournful drunk
(Or is that us?) with every number;
Bill's now acquired non-smoker's cough.
Perhaps it's time that we were off.

Ismailovo, where Tsars once hunted,
And Peter messed about in boats,
And avant-garde art once confronted
The power of men in long white coats,
Is now a heaven for bargain-hunters,
(And hell for all unwary punters),
A car-boot-Disney paradise
Where History will find its price
As long as somebody is willing
To haggle for these toy *Salyuts*,
Those Soviet Army surplus boots,
And someone somewhere makes a killing
To serve that brave and noble cause,
Flea-market economic laws.

Today's the first lie-in for ages.
Outside someone is sweeping snow.
We turn the pavement's virgin pages
To slush and mud. Today we go
To Mayakovsky's house, all bloody
With art and history; the study
Where he committed suicide
And something more than one man died.
Tonight we sit at separate tables
To keep the schools of poets apart;
We separate the world from art,
Mistaking one another's labels;
When one describes his work as 'stuff!'
Turns out he meant to say, 'It's tough!'

Some kindergarten kids are playing
At statues in the freezing rain
Among the fallen heads decaying
Outside the Tretyakov; a lane
Of ten-pin Easter Island skittles
(No Gorbachov!) Thus time belittles
All those who fall like dominoes
(One pock-marked Stalin's lost his nose).
We argue later on the Metro
About which leader-cult's more kitsch –
Dzerzhinsky or Abramovich?
Or black-belt Putin-Stalin retro?
At Bukberi we're asked to scrawl
Our signatures upon the wall.

At Sheremetyevo our pent up
Desire to purchase Russian tat's
Soon satisfied until we've spent up
On duty-free and furry hats;
Although it's not the stuff for purists,
We're going home dressed up as tourists!
This time we're flying wrong way round,
Against the clock, but homeward bound,
And feel the tug of Anglophilia
When drifts of snow-clouds part to show
The planet turning green below;
A strange and welcome sight, familiar
As any well-loved, clichéd poem
Whose last line always rhymes with home.

Idiot Snow

for Sergei, Yuri and Olga

This sky's a foreign language
  Whose native speakers know
It takes the earth's thesaurus
  To catch the falling snow.
As well as try translating
  The way the weather talks –
In Russian verbs of motion
  Snow doesn't fall, it *walks*.
It ambles, shambles, gambols,
  It sidles, idles, creeps,
It bounces, pounces, flounces,
  It pirouettes and leaps,
It does the hokey-cokey,
  The twist, the cha-cha-cha
In a silent karaoke
  In Snegurochka's Bar.

Small children play at statues
  Outside the ice-carved shops
Till everybody freezes,
  And when the music stops
The speechless world is deafened
  By the ringing in our ears
Like underwater singing
  Or the music of the spheres.
The sound of snowflakes walking
  Through Kemerovo at night
Would silence anyone who doubts
  That happiness writes white,
The colour of the senses
  At ten degrees below,
Where no matter what the question is,
  The answer's always snow.

Idiot Bag

for Zhenya and Natalya

Well the hotel room's too narrow
And the bed settee's too wide,
The radiator's boiling
And it's -10 outside,
And I'm trying to work the telly
While I try to understand
What I'm doing in Siberia
When my bag's in Samarkand.

The naked light-bulb's hanging
From the ceiling by a thread,
My body-clock alarm goes off
When I should be in bed,
So I'm trying to use this mobile
While I sit here and lament
The fact I'm in Siberia
But my bag is in Tashkent.

The toilet-seat is broken
And the shower blows cold and hot,
The clothes that I am wearing
Are the only ones I've got,
So I'd better wash this T-shirt
While I try to work out why
I'm stuck here in Siberia
While my bag is in Dubai.

I thought that I was miserable
But now I've heard the news –
Croatia's beaten England,
And I've got those homesick blues;
That's it – I'm going to pack my bag
And catch the next flight home,
Except I'm in Siberia
And my bag is now in Rome.

Lesson

'I will work hard,' said the boy,
'I will wait for you,' said his mother,
'I will shoot you,' hissed the bullet.

'I will keep you warm,' said the wall,
'I will keep you dry,' said the roof,
'I will burn you,' roared the fire.

'I will help you,' said the teacher,
'I will be your friend,' said the girl,
'I will crush you,' cried the ruins.

'I will make you smile,' said the funny drawing,
'I will make you jump,' said the basket-ball hoop,
'I will bury you,' whispered the blood.

'I will rescue you,' said the soldier,
'I will be strong,' said the president,
'I will be stronger,' said the voice in the dark.

And the world span round, like a basket-ball,
And everyone did as they said they would,
And children, teachers, friends, roof, wall,
Met bullets, ruins, fire and blood.

And when it came to a stop inside the hall
We understood the difference between
All those who promise what they mean
And those who mean nothing at all.

V

'For some, prison is the university of time, a great think tank of crime and human circumstance, most of it tragic, a vast library of unwritten biographies and stories. Here are the plots of elaborate grabs and swindles, daring and imaginative frauds, tales of detection and discovery, cops and robbers, the ravelling and unravelling of mysteries.'

Ken Smith, *Inside Time*

The Ballad of Writing Gaol

'Some with a flattering word.'
Oscar Wilde

for Clive Hopwood and Pauline Bennett

In Holme House gaol by Stockton town
   The pads are strangely quiet;
It's not the zonked-out slumber of
   The usual H-plan diet,
But something in the air just like
   The hush before a riot.

The telephones are silent where
   There's usually noisy queues,
The Listeners have all shut their ears
   To other people's blues,
And no-one's listening to a game
   The Boro mustn't lose.

There's something going on that can't
   Be easily explained:
A mass break-out of gentleness
   And passion unrestrained,
An outbreak of Testosterone
   And tenderness regained.

Instead of using library books
   For toilet rolls and roaches,
The guys are busy studying
   To deal with love's reproaches,
To learn their answers off by heart
   As Feb 14th approaches.

For even those who think they're hard
    Must honour love's own laws,
And sack their pads for similes
    That serve the lover's cause,
For metaphors and metonyms
    In praise of her outdoors.

Between Dear John and Child Support,
    Ex-girlfriends and ex-wives,
Between bang-up and breakfast-time,
    In dreams of other lives,
Each man soon learns that even here
    The need for love survives.

Though tattooed names can be erased,
    And proudest lovers wilt,
One kiss and you are in for Life,
    You're in right to the hilt;
Love offers no remission
    From innocence or guilt.

So the warriors at the windows stand
    And silently rehearse
The sugared phrases which they hope
    At least won't make things worse,
And suck their honeyed words until
    They find they've written verse.

There's poets on the landings,
    And there's lovers on remand,
There's lines of poetry up for grabs
    In smuggled contraband,
While those who're good at free verse find
    Themselves in much demand.

On House Block 1 and House Block 2
    They've all turned balladeer;
The rhythms start to rattle
    As the haze begins to clear,
They do their cluck and ride their bikes
    To get their rhymes in gear.

If – as the song says – love's a drug,
    Who needs a bag of smack?
When love's the strongest buzz you know,
    There's not much call for crack,
And nothing beats the rush of first
    Love's aphrodisiac.

The lads on Houseblock 3 and 4
    Joy-ride their new sestinas,
There's polished sonnets up on 5
    Well-buffed by landing cleaners,
On 6 they watch repeats of old
    Romantic misdemeanours.

And in the prison library
    The poetry shelves are barren,
For even love poems have their price
    Set by some baccy baron
(Who needs a quick Black Lace when you've
    A Sapphic to your Sharon?)

There's some who sit up half the night
    And do their very best
To get their lass upon the page
    And off their tattooed chest,
In poetry that's as rigorous
    As any urine test.

It isn't easy writing when
    Your heart is in the dock,
But you can write in solitude
    From bang-up to unlock
(And there's so many poets in Seg
    It's known as Writer's Block!)

When visits are so public
    And letters are so prized,
The heightened truths of poetry
    Are not to be despised:
What's hard to say in plainer words
    In art is undisguised.

Because the need for love's a truth
    More desperate in the Slammer,
All those who have been starved so long
    Of tenderness and glamour,
Create a common art that speaks
    In love's peculiar grammar.

I love you, babe, *ich liebe dich*,
    Sound weak and lachrymose,
Je t'aime's been said so many times
    In poetry and prose.
But *odi et amo*'s still true,
    A rose is still a rose.

The images in magazines
    May make some feel quite fruity,
But any man who kneels before
    His shrine to female Beauty
Soon learns such rituals are a sad
    And solitary duty;

The otherness of women melts
    Before such yearning fire,
Creates a burning myth of love,
    A bonfire of desire,
On which the slaves of Venus
    Must burn a world entire.

In all the clichéd, second-hand
    And sentimental tropes,
Each unconvincing chat-up line
    Once heard on TV soaps,
You hear the brittle sound of little,
    Fragile human hopes.

Though Valentine's the patron saint
    Of young hearts everywhere,
This festival contains a truth
    In which all mortals share:
That someone loves us still's the hope
    That keeps us from despair.

And here, where every letter home
    And billet-doux's policed,
The poetry of every man
    This Valentine's Day feast,
Asserts that art, like hope and love
    Cannot stay unreleased.

Black and Blue

for Gary

He wears his war-paint like a skin,
  An Ancient Briton dipped in woad,
A pirate, an Apache chief,
  A child whose face-paint's overflowed.
There's tattoos on his neck and hands,
  There's sketches etched upon his back,
His face is like a book engraved
  In biro blue and needle black.
His legs and arms are indigo,
  His skin is scored in black and blue,
An inky web embroidery –
  The man's a walking, live tattoo!

His body's like a map of pain,
  Whose shores are lined in bold tattoos,
The sapphire statue of a man
  That's chiselled from a purple bruise.
The overall effect's designed
  To say that blue-black blokes are scary,
A warning sign for wary folk
  Announcing *noli me tangere*.
But who can say what lies beneath
  The diamond patina of art,
And who can guess the colour of
  A naked, soft, unpainted heart?

Villain-elle

'Mature poets steal.'
  T.S. Eliot

It doesn't matter if you cannot spell,
And plagiarism's not a serious crime
When you are writing in a prison cell.

Who gives a toss about the Prize Nobel,
The ladders up which un-barred bards can climb?
It doesn't matter if you cannot spell,

The individual doesn't stand out well
Among so many poets doing time.
When you are writing in a prison cell

It's sometimes rather difficult to tell
Which is a found and which a stolen rhyme.
It doesn't matter. If you cannot spell

There's always those who are prepared to sell
A smuggled rap or line at bang-up time
When you are writing in a prison cell.

Because such second-hand materiel
Is that which makes all common art sublime,
It doesn't matter if you cannot spell
When you are writing in a prison cell.

Honest

D'you hear the one about the lad
   Whose head was full of sawdust things,
Who broke the heart of his old Dad,
   Who danced while others pulled his strings,
Whose life was one long holiday,
Who lost his conscience on the way?

The muppet who – I kid you not –
   Chose Pleasure Island over school,
Who didn't think that fire was hot,
   Who kicked off like a braying mule,
Who never seemed to realise
He couldn't hide his wooden lies?

Swear down – though it may sound bizarre,
   The jackass taken for a ride
Who wished upon a shooting star
   But found himself banged-up inside
The belly of a monstrous whale
Is not, round here, a fairy-tale.

This is the realm of alibis,
   Of dodgy tales and ancient gags,
Of lame excuses, stale pork pies,
   Unlikely boasts and epic blags,
But none is more familiar than
The boy who would become a man.

The only part that's hard to follow
   Is where he sheds his Midas ears;
A happy ending's hard to swallow
   For those whose stories end in tears.
Not every moral has a story.
Yeah right. Whatever. Jackanory.

How Do You Spell Heroin?

Call me unreconstructed if you like,
  But if you really want to fry your brains,
If you like riding backwards on your bike
  And pumping brown and brick-dust in your veins,
If you intend to do another cluck
  Until your rattling bones begin to melt,
If you're prepared to ache and feel like fuck –
  At least you should know how the stuff is spelled.

Of course there's things you cannot learn at school,
  And smack's now less a verb and more a noun,
And pedantry is never ever cool,
  But there's some things that can't be written down:
And not because they can't be said – far from it –
It's just they're best expressed in blood and vomit.

Form

for Hilary and Andrea

Induction, first thing Monday morning.
   The library's full of spaced-out lads,
Hung-over, rattling, bruised and yawning,
   Exploring life outside their pads.
Their first long Monday back in gaol,
   Most look as if they haven't slept;
There's always one though, without fail,
   Will ask me where the *poetry*'s kept.

He knows that he must write a letter
   Explaining what went wrong this time,
And somehow thinks regret sounds better
   Expressed in someone else's rhyme;
Though why should anyone suppose
   That poetry makes the best excuses,
I can't imagine – still, it shows
   That even poets have their uses.

He skips the modern stuff of course –
   Too *personal*, hard work, unclear;
The awkward syntax of remorse
   Needs more if it's to sound sincere –
A common music whose appeal
   Is that it speaks for everyone,
The patterned language of the real
   That's usually written by Anon.

Chaotic lives require some form,
   And in the middle of the night
The fires that keep all humans warm
   Need more than words to stay alight.
But who can tell the reason why
   A promise made so many times
It's polished as a well-worn lie
   Sounds more convincing when it rhymes?

Team Strip

The gym screws always pick up sides,
  One team in bibs, the other skins,
A game defined by reckless slides,
  By battered pride and battered shins,
A weekly work-out down the gym
  That's GBH in all but name,
Where players risk both life and limb
  To prove it's more than just a game.

But later, in the changing rooms
  Hostilities are put aside.
The game's forgotten. Life resumes,
  Aggression's hunger satisfied.
We strip down to a uniform
  Of tattooed muscle, fat and hair,
The unembarrassed, classless norm
  Of sweaty maleness anywhere.
A line of pink and noisy blokes
  Beneath the shower's half-hearted spray,
We swap the usual Makkem jokes
  And scrub the prison-stink away;
Exchanging stories of the lives
  We left behind us at the gate,
Imagined children, girlfriends, wives,
  Half-hearted dreams of going straight.
The perfect job. A life of ease.
  Time we were gone; it's ten past one,
And time for work. We get our keys,
  Remembering which side we're on.

Zoology

Beware the wolves who hunt in packs,
   The snake's insinuating smile,
The low-browed, strong-armed silverbacks,
   The sympathetic crocodile;
Avoid the vultures' scrounging gaze
   The tiger playing with his food,
The magpie's flashy, thieving ways,
   The leopard in a hungry mood;
Beware the lizards' sleepless eyes,
   The grizzly dozing in the straw,
The piglets rooting in their sties,
   The jungle stink of carnivore;
Stay clear of keepers jangling keys,
   The crazy dogs who bark at night,
The laughter of the chimpanzees,
   The paws that scratch, the jaws that bite.

But most of all, beware the law
   That rattles at the window bars,
The food-chain red in tooth and claw
   Of those that hunt beneath the stars,
The moon-lit siren calls of home
   Which draw all creatures great and small
To where those midnight monsters roam
   That lie in wait, beyond the wall.

Away!

for Harry Ashby

It's raining on the walkway's metal roof,
    Inside and out, another freezing day,
And yet this notice-board's a kind of proof
    That somewhere skies are warm and blue, not grey.
This postcard collage throbs with endless blues
    From cloudless skies in Sicily and Spain,
The kind of blues you do not want to lose
    (Especially when the day is grey with rain),
From far-off lands of olive, sun and grape,
To which each year we make our great escape.

These postcards sent from Turkey and Corfu,
    Illegible, stamped, faded, always late,
Are like the letters sent by Lifers who
    Believe that there's still life beyond the Gate,
Utopians, Believers, Dreamers all,
    Who think that dreams of freedom might come true,
Whose dreams are pinned up on the staff-room wall
    For all to see – a shrine, a tent of blue,
A sun-lit summer's day, a cloudless shape,
A blur of sky, a vision of escape.

And so we dig our tunnels in our heads,
    Emerging in the sunlight once a year
To scribble messages that, though unread,
    Say simply that we're there, instead of here,
But long before they reach us from Australia,
    Sardinia, Peru or Singapore,
We're back inside again, the system's failures –
    Once out we keep on coming back for more,
Because no matter how you scrimp and scrape,
This place is one from which there's no escape . . .

VI

'*You speak of the* Charms *of Southwell; the* Place *I* abhor. *The Fact is I remain here because I can appear no where else, being* completely done *up.* Wine *and* Women *have* dished *your* humble Servant, *not a* Sou *to be* had; *all* over; *condemned to exist (I cannot say live) at this* Crater *of Dullness till my* Lease *of* Infancy *expires.*'

Byron to John Hanson, 2 April 1807

Either or Eyether

for Ross Bradshaw

Some people call a spade a spade,
   And some a bloody shovel,
Some call this village *Sou*thwell, while
   There's those who call it *Su*thwell.
Pronouncing English place-names is
   A weird linguistic test
That separates the world between
   The locals and the rest.

Come friendly bombs and drop on Slough
   (Which doesn't sound like Hough,
Though Mousehole and Newcastle rhyme,
   Like Wild Boar Clough and Burgh).
From Slathwaite, Meols and Potter Heigham,
   From Stiffkey up to Alnwick
So many place-names seem designed
   To put us in a panic.

Unless you want to look a fool
   Avoid the Vale of Belvoir,
Don't go to Bicester or to Fowey,
   Skip Ulgham, Rothwell and Peover.
You won't get any reading done
   In Reading, and per*lease*,
Don't ask the way to Magdalene
   To Pelby or to Caius.

It's sometimes said that English ears
   Think most things rhyme with class,
(That's why we either sound just like
   An arse or else an ass).
In England when you speak you put
   Your foot inside your mouth,
In Southwell, though, nobody cares
   If you say Suth or South.

Deriving from Old English 'suth',
　Itself from 'sunth', or sunny,
The first half of this name suggests
　A land of milk and honey.
And so it is – well, of a sort:
　While others would divide us
By how we speak, here no-one knows
　The natives from outsiders.

I like a place that can't agree
　On how to say its name,
Such splendid indecisiveness
　Should be your claim to fame;
I'm off back now to Middlesbrough,
　(Which nobody can spell),
So whether you are South or Suth
　I wish this village well.

Faith: Southwell Minster

When the Ironsides stabled their horses in here
   They were acting upon the belief
That the cry of the Lord could be heard more clear
   In straw than in scriptured gold leaf.
         Though a temple is built
         Of stained-glass and gilt
It's foundations are laid in the levelling fear
   That all faiths, in the end, come to grief.

Hope: Southwell Races

In the anapaest thunder of sinew and nerve,
  There's a magic more strong than the bet
That will earn us a fortune if only we serve
  At the altar of muscle and sweat.
        But though everyone wants
        To imagine just once
That our fortune is earned, that it's what we deserve,
  We all know we deserve what we get.

Charity: Southwell Workhouse

If you follow this straight, narrow pathway it leads
  To a mansion with only one door.
Here Love profited greatly by meeting the needs
  Of Society, Money and Law.
        Though it beareth all things,
        True charity springs
From the knowledge that nobody ever succeeds
  In escaping the house of the poor.

Little Green Men

It is hard not to think that there's something obscene
  In these nine leering heads carved in stone,
Something feral, repressed, australopithecine,
    An invisible friend we've out-grown.
          But supposing we found
          It's the other way round:
That our pre-human nature, still grinning and green,
  Is about to come into its own?

VII

'We consider the town hall one of the finest specimens of shed-architecture, extant; it is a combination of the pig-stye and tea-garden-box orders . . . Seated on the massive wooden benche . . . the sage men of Mudfog spend hour after hour in grave deliberation. Here they settle at what hour of the night public houses shall be closed, at what hour of the morning they shall be permitted to open, how soon it shall be lawful for people to eat their dinner on church-days, and other great political questions; and sometimes, long after silence has fallen on the town, and the distant lights from the shops and houses have ceased to twinkle, like far-off stars, to the sight of the boatmen on the river, the illumination in the two unequal-sized windows of the town hall, warns the inhabitants of Mudfog that its little body of legislators, like a larger and better-known body of the same genus, a great deal more noisy, and not a whit more profound, are patriotically dozing away in company, far into the night, for their country's good.'

Charles Dickens

A Question of History

The Lambton Worm is stirring in the mud,
  In Stanhope fairies dance in mushroom rings,
The Brancepeth Brawn's been sighted in the wood,
  The A1 Angel flaps its rusty wings,
Peg Powler wakes beneath the River Tees,
  The tide is coming in at Morpeth town,
The Monkey's swinging through the Headland trees,
  The Cauld Lad's turned the whole world upside down.

At Stainmore, Eric Bloodaxe swings his axe,
  In Stanwick, Cartimandua still reigns,
The ghosts of pits and docks and railway tracks,
  Of furnaces and shipyards shake their chains.
It's said that History's stirring in the North.
What kind it is, we'll see November fourth.

A Theory of Devolution

'The Everlasting No.'
  Thomas Carlyle

O Archaeology! The precious art
Whose digging sets the human race apart,
The science that shows our footprints in the mud
Like Hansel's pebbles in the moonlit wood,
That lights our upward path and shows us how
We made our painful climb from then to now,
The muddy narrative in which we trace
The noble story of the human race
Whose progress would make even Darwin blush –
From chimpanzee to President George Bush.

But archaeology has lately shown
That *Homo Sapiens* is not alone!
That humankind's ascent has been defined
By leaving awkward relatives behind.
Reports are coming in of curious sightings
Of something only found in Tolkein's writings –
A mythical and long-forgotten type
Of little brain (you've probably read the hype).
Homo Hyperboreus is its name,
A long-lost pawn in evolution's game,
A quiet race, a tribe of Northern creatures
Distinguished by their awful Northern features:
One angel, several whippets, Hovis ads,
Pollution, Andy Capp, *The Likely Lads*,
The Gallowgate, brown ale and giro-cheques –
An ethnic group of stunted Ant and Decs
Resembling hobbits, trolls and chimpanzees
Who dwelt between the rivers Tweed and Tees.

No doubt their lives were nasty, brute and short,
Incapable, it seems, of proper thought,
And yet there is a puzzle still unsolved
If we're to know just how these folk devolved
Concerning certain well-preserved remains
That indicate they tried to use their brains!
Cave paintings show they wore a troubled crown,
Receding foreheads furrowed by a frown
Suggesting they were puzzled by some query
Too difficult for those not used to theory.
Just what this question was remains unclear,
But it seems linked to artefacts found near
Their primitive and simple dwelling places.
Forensic tests on these have found the traces
Of marks describing (this is our best guess)
A set of simple words like 'No' and 'Yes'.
Though future scholarship may yet reveal
The question which their 'Yes' and 'No' conceal,
Such riddles seemed to shape their culture (*viz*
Their taste for something known as the 'pub quiz').
Who knows what their significance might be?
Our anthropologists cannot agree
What kind of savage game they once expressed:
A fight maybe? A race? A sexual test?
Perhaps some strange religious merchandise
Connected to a ritual sacrifice?
Or else a kind of childish art denoting
The cult of origami postal-voting?

One school believes these artefacts must show
Two rival deities called 'Yes' and 'No',
One representing spring and life and bread,
And one the wintry kingdom of the dead.
Apparently each rival god could claim
A multitude to worship in its name;
The objects found beside their cave-mouth fires
Include weird badges, coffee-mugs and flyers,
Car-window stickers, T-shirts, campaign posters,
Umbrellas, baseball-caps, balloons and coasters,
One large white elephant, one furry mouse
(Totemic structure – *cf* Lévi-Strauss).

On late-night TV slots and phone-in shows
All those who followed Yes would fight with Nos,
While campaign caravans and battle buses
Tried teaching all the minuses and pluses
Of their own gods to those who didn't know
Which deity to pray for, Yes or No.

Mnemosyne! thou guardian of the vast
And speechless desert sands we call the past,
Show us the way to better understand
The secrets of these footprints in the sand
And why they so abruptly disappear
Somewhere beside the rivers Tyne and Wear.
One theory is they'd reached that Kubrick stage
When human cultures either come of age
(Cue Nietzsche, Richard Strauss and Zoroasater)
Or else give up a fate they cannot master.
It seems these folk began to retrogress
When those who worshipped No defeated Yes
And that the reign of No is clearly linked
To why these Northern folk are now extinct.
While followers of Yes-ness perished first,
The cult of No-ness could not be reversed.
Unstoppable as any cliff-bound lemming,
Their self-destructive habit of condemning
The risk of any future but the last
Prevented them escaping from the past.

Instead of standing tall beneath the trees
They crawled away to pick each other's fleas.
Like something from a page of Friedrich Nietzsche's,
This dwindling Morlock race of Northern creatures
Climbed down the human family tree and laid
Their sorry heads beneath its spreading shade
Until a dashing Indiana Jones
Discovered some familiar-looking bones
Inside a newly-excavated trench;
A kind of cuddly hobbit *untermensch*
Afraid of change, afraid of life itself,
A false-start left on Evolution's shelf.

All this is clear to experts holding forth
About the savage culture of the North,
Who argue that these folk were bound to fail
So far from London's civilising pale,
Who find in every clue, however small,
The proof the North's not human after all.
There's others, though, who think the problem's harder,
That what occurred at this Bag End-Masada,
This tragedy of dodo-like proportion,
Requires that we proceed with greater caution.
Unlikely though it seems, we must pursue
The thought that they were just like me and you.
The dread of change is not, as History shows,
Confined to those who have prehensile toes.
The past will always lay its hairy hand
On futures that it cannot understand
So long as we let monkey fears perplex us
From windy Hartlepool to sunny Texas.

Dirty Work in Mudfog

I saw some ships come sailing by
  On Christmas Day, on Christmas Day,
I saw some ships come sailing by
  Across the ocean blue.
And those ships they were a ghostly sight,
  A ghastly sight, a terrible sight,
They sailed at night by an eerie light
  And were sailed by a skeleton crew.

And when the people saw this thing,
  This zombie thing, this haunted thing,
And knew what cargo it did bring,
  Their hearts were sore afraid.
But what was on these thirteen ships,
  These phantom ships, these coffin-ships?
What freight malign on this graveyard line
  Did this ghost fleet bring to trade?

Why did they sail to Mudfog Town,
  To Mudfog Town, to Mudfog Town?
What did they here with their cargo of fear?
  O why does nobody answer?
The ships were built of toxic waste,
  Asbestos waste and diesel waste,
And PCBs that cause disease,
  For the ships were riddled with cancer.

And they sailed away for a year and a day,
  From a toxic kingdom far away,
And they sailed away through the ocean spray,
  So someone could make a buck.
But they say that money's a curious thing,
  A puzzling thing, a mysterious thing,
How rarely it goes to any of those
  Who are left to clear up the muck.

And so the thirteen ships sailed on
    To Mudfog Town, to Mudfog Town,
Where the dirt will stay when the money's away
    Dancing across the waves.
And all the souls on earth shall sing,
    And all the bells on earth shall ring,
And all the angels in Heav'n shall sing,
    Above our children's graves.

Live From Revolution Square, Mudfogistan

We watch as crowds in Kiev brave the cold,
  And Georgians chase their government away,
We cheer the young who stand up to the old
  And strive to make each day the First of May.
In Myanmar, Ukraine and Kyrgysztan,
  The spirit of revolt is now abroad,
As angry crowds proclaim the rights of Man,
  And prove that voting's mightier than the sword.

From Bishek, Belgrade, Minsk and Uruguay
  We praise the spring-time dream of revolution,
And rarely pause to ask ourselves just why
  Elections here are always Lilliputian.
And yet, although our leaders all contrive
  To stop the revolution's horse from bolting,
The spirit of revolt here's still alive –
  In Britain *all* the parties are revolting.

Human Estate

Below these hills, beneath the sky,
   Above this iron-age town,
We march all day and wonder why
   We're neither up nor down.
This muddy footpath marks the way
   That leads you down the street;
But who can say whose feet of clay
   Once walked beneath your feet?

As pilgrims through this world we pass,
   Like children in a wood,
And though one foot is on the gas
   The other's caked in mud.
Down Dixon's Bank the road descends
   Then climbs back to the top;
But who knows where their journey ends,
   Or when the road will stop?

The Roman village whose remains
   Beneath the path you tread's
The deep foundation that sustains
   The roof above your heads.
An entrance and an exit might
   Seem opposite by name;
But who is sure which one is right
   When all roads look the same?

And deeper still are buried scars,
   The finger-prints that show
How tall we stood beneath the stars
   Two thousand years ago.
These marks upon the pavement's page
   Are neither mine nor yours;
But who can't still recall the age
   When they ran on all fours?

How hard it is to contemplate
    Those cold and barefoot lives,
And yet in this new-built estate
    The will to build survives.
A foot that isn't wearing shoes
    May leave a modest hollow;
But which of us can ever choose
    The footsteps we must follow?

The present is a building site,
    A future unfulfilled;
 The deeper our foundations lie,
    The higher we can build.
They thought two thousand years ago
    That all roads led to Rome,
But weary travellers always know
    That all roads lead us home.

Red Ellen

'Middlesbrough is a book of illustrations to Karl Marx.'
Ellen Wilkinson, 1924

She stares out from the pages of *New Dawn*
   As though the future needs to be out-faced,
   Her flaming red-flag tresses to her waist
Among the endless fields of unripe corn.
They christened her Red Ellen, Little Nell,
   Miss Perky, Fiery Atom, Little Minx,
   As if to say this cold, old world still thinks
All fiery reds are burning brands from hell.

   In Jarrow and in Middlesbrough today
The flames of change are embers in the grate,
Cold fires of ash and dust that illustrate
   How much we all prefer the colour grey,
Still too distracted by the colour red
To see the fire that's waiting to be fed.

This Is Not a Poem

'When Nations grow Old. The Arts grow Cold.
And Commerce settles on every Tree.'
  William Blake

What verse-form better than *ottava rima*,
  That model of tradition and technique,
To celebrate the opening at mima
  Of major British artists' work last week?
That wasn't, by the way, an *erotema*
  (A question with no answer – from the Greek),
If too much craft can make an art that's heartless,
It's also true too little can be artless.

Within these bright and airy, sunless halls
  Are hung the very wonders of our age:
Mysterious dots and scribbles on the walls,
  Self-advertising dribbles on the page,
Illegible as Palaeolithic scrawls,
  Unsympathetic magic to engage
The low-life creatures of creation myths,
Like Patrick Brill and his old friends the Smiths.

This poem's not a pipe, it is a bowl,
  A fruitless poem no-one understands
Since nobody can read it. Very droll.
  This bundle of decaying rubber-bands
Is not a stone. It seems that on the whole
  The old gags are the best. The age demands
That I should save myself a lot of work
And simply sign my name, like Gavin Turk.

The value of this art lies in the bank
  And not in common, shared, collective craft;
Some canvases are maybe better blank,
  And every poem needs another draft,
As this one does, but if I may be frank,
  I can't be bothered putting in the graft,
And anyway, this poem's overdue.
O sod technique – er, Sandra, will this do?

VIII

Too Much

in memoriam Geoff Croft

You always were too big, too tall, too loud,
   The sort of man who took up too much space,
Who couldn't help but stand out in a crowd,
   The kind of Dad who was always on my case,
But as I watched you whittled with each breath,
   Belittled by both cancer and its cure,
   I needed you still louder than before,
As large as life and larger still than death.

You always were too big, too loud, too tall,
   The sort of man who never seemed to stop,
Beside whom other fathers seemed so small,
   The kind of Dad they'd call over the top.
But as I watched you lying there so still,
   I could not fail to understand the size
   Of what I've lost in you, to realise
How huge a gap you've left for me to fill.

By Heart

for Jean Croft at 80

The longest lives can sometimes seem defined
   By words like grandma, mother, daughter, wife –
Supporting roles which, when they are combined,
   Suggest perhaps a kind of back-stage life.
And yet we know the opposite is true,
   That as we try to learn our lines we find
   Within the parts we too have been assigned
How much our lives have been defined by you.

Whatever

for Al at 18

'Whatever, Dad,' you shrug, as if to say
   You haven't heard, or else could not care less;
Whatever number you are asked to play
   You wear with such conspicuous success;
Whatever you've attempted, you have done;
    Whatever sport, you're on the winning side.
    And yet, whatever future you decide,
To me you'll always be my youngest son.

Go!

for Charl at 18

You always knew just how to time a run:
   While others hared away, you kept your pace
To finish with such confidence and grace,
   The tortoise who invariably won.
So now we watch with confidence and pride
   As you train for a different kind of race;
   No matter what the hurdles you will face
We know that you'll take winning in your stride.

Checkpoint Charlie

for Charlie Wilson

You can grow a tache like Dali,
Clank your chains like Jacob Marley,
You can learn to speak Bengali,
Look for polar bears on Bali,
Be a rebel like Steve Harley;
You can wave your arms like Kali,
Quench your thirst with lemon-barley
In the desert sands of Mali,
Sing *The Internationale*
In Somali or Gurkhali;
You can celebrate Diwali
In the barrios of Cali,
Get a tattoo in Kigali,
Try to act like Joe Pasquale,
In the slums of Mexicali –
But no matter how bizarrely
You act
It's a fact
There's only one proper Charlie.

Foggiest

for Emma Metcalfe

I awoke in a fog
But the fog was too thick,
Yes the fog was so thick
All I saw was the fog.

Caught a flight in the fog
But the fog was too thick,
Yes the fog was so thick
Couldn't land in the fog.

I was stuck in the fog
For the fog was too thick,
Yes the fog was so thick
I was stuck in the fog.

Caught a bus in the fog
But the fog was too thick,
Yes the fog was so thick
Couldn't shift in the fog.

Couldn't think for the fog
For the fog was too thick,
Yes the fog was so thick
I was sick of the fog.

I got home in the fog
But the fog was as thick
As a man who would fly
Down to Bath in thick fog.

They Think It's All Over

And so our first group-game is finished,
Another World Cup tale begins.
With optimism undiminished
We hope that this time England wins,
And that just maybe Peter Crouch is
The man to pin us to our couches,
And end the forty years of hurt
That comes with every England shirt.
And yet there can be few supporters
Who really are in any doubt
About the way this will turn out;
By now experience has taught us
That hope's a dangerous burden, which
Has no place on a football pitch.

The wrong side of the years of plenty,
We make the best of what remains;
With luck, for me, another twenty –
At least five more World Cup campaigns!
Although I don't think for one minute
That's long enough for us to win it,
I've long learned how to live in hope
(How else could I have learned to cope
With Englishness?) The generation
That still remembers Moore and Hurst,
Who've grown up to expect the worst
Can sometimes fall for the temptation
To mistake England for the fans
Whose tabloid colours deck their vans.

For those who landed on the planet
In '56, we chose a time
In which, no matter how you scan it
A word like Victory just won't rhyme.
Five decades of imperial slaughter
Is quite enough for this supporter;
From Suez Crisis to Iraq
Old England's never lost the knack
Of picking fights with Third World nations.
A grisly time in which to spend
One's time on earth. I can't pretend
That there are many consolations –
At least as far as I can tell –
Except my friends were here as well.

I'm probably suffering from depression,
Brought on by turning one more page
In life's thin book, but my impression
Is that my friends don't seem to age.
My oldest mates are always youthful –
No, please don't laugh – I'm being truthful!
Still hanging round in student pubs,
In parties, staff-rooms, classes, Cubs,
In Sunday school and Party meeting,
On five-a-side courts, clapped-out cars,
In prison, readings, Russian bars –
Though art is long and life is fleeting,
There's few things that can measure us
The way that friendship's time-piece does.

I'm glad that you've been here to share it.
Without such friends, it would have been
Impossible sometimes to bear it.
A half a century lived between
High expectation and disaster
Is more than any one can master.
The years spent watching England play
And all we've won is sweet F.A.
And yet within this summer garden
There is another England here,
Defined by comradeship and beer;
My country's here, not Baden-Baden,
With you, the friends who'll cheer me up –
When England exits the World Cup.

June 2006

Clerihew and Cry

George Bush
Is not in a rush
To pardon
Bin Laden.

Tony Blair
Doesn't care
How many fibs
He ad-libs.

Jack Straw
Imagines war
Like a lawyer,
Not a Goya.

The press condemns
Those WMDs,
Although tabloid dailies
Ignore the Israelis'.

If anyone's more sinister
Than the British Prime Minister
The US neo-cons
Are the ones.

Rumsfeld and Cheney
Think they are brainy;
But pride and cupidity
Looks just like stupidity.

The Pentagon
Admires Ariel Sharon,
But they entertain low opinions
Of the rights of Palestinians.

Iraq may be freed
But all are agreed
The carnage in Fallujah
Gets huger.

London civilians
Protest in their millions;
We want the troops back
From Iraq.

Not So

in memoriam Julia Darling

The rules are fixed. We can't compete with you.
   Before we start we know the final score.
Of course you win. The powerful always do.
   You are the offside goal, the final straw.
No doubt you like to think you're really hard,
   Tooled up with cluster bomb and DU shell;
All we possess is mortal love and art
   While you with poison, war and sickness dwell.
But look at you – old morgue-faced charnel-breath,
   Still trying to play the vampire when we know
You're just a hammy Hammer-horror show.
   Poor you. It's living that is hard, not death.
And Julia's art and love will both survive
Her being dead, by being so alive.

IX

Letter to Randall Swingler Part III

for Deborah Rogers

I know I said that once your Life was out
 The pair of us could go our separate ways;
My hopes of fame and fortune up the spout
 I'd write instead the kind of book that pays,
While you could rest in peace again without
 Being pestered by my questions or my praise.
(So many years of working in your shadow
Was turning me into a right old saddo.)

Alas, it didn't quite work out as I'd planned.
 The walk-on parts which Fortune has assigned us
Mark out our way like footsteps in the sand
 Then vanish as the tide comes in behind us.
Like castaways who think we've reached dry land
 Too late we find Leviathan's undermined us.
I'm writing this somewhere inside the whale
That swinges the volumes of its horrid flail.

It's true I said I wouldn't write again,
 That two unanswered letters were enough,
(Was it too much to hope that you might pen
 A few quick lines?) but please don't take the huff,
There's reasons why I've got this sudden yen
 To write again. If you don't like it – tough.
A few more verses, mate, and then we're through.
But first of all – have I got news for you . . .

This is the title of a TV series
 Which puts our politicians in the stocks,
The kind of show of which one quickly wearies
 Because the very monsters which it mocks
Have sussed committing public hara-kiri's
 A sassy way to get them on the box.
Thus comedy's employed to render affable
A politics that isn't really laughable.

As someone said (I think it was Quintilian)
    Some kinds of laughter cost too much. The wars
We fight these days are costed by the billion;
    The price of breaching international laws
Is paid for by the dead (mostly civilian);
    And yet unlike that total war of yours,
Death's sound-track these days isn't quite so martial –
Our doctrine isn't total-war, but *partial*.

You see we've learned to live our daily lives
    As though these daily slaughters don't deplete us;
Just like a herd of zebra that contrives
    To look away while one's devoured by cheetahs,
We keep our heads down till the day arrives
    When no-one else is left. And so they eat us.
That zebras never turn on their pursuers
Is quickly understood by TV viewers.

The fact we find such natural history thrilling
    When living in an age of endless war,
That we don't mind being shown a lot of killing
    As long as it's performed by carnivore,
Suggests that we are still, alas, more willing
    To think that Nature's red in tooth and claw
Than to confront the *truly* scary creatures –
By which I mean the ones with human features.

The rule of Endless War's now set in marble,
    A policy we dimly apprehend
Must mean the deaths in Baghdad and in Kabul,
    The secret torture camps which they pretend
To justify with all the usual garble
    About defending Freedom, will not end
Until, as Khrushchev put it, shrimps can whistle.
Which brings me to the point of this epistle.

By which I'm not referring to our book,
    Though if you really want, I'll tell you quickly:
It came and went, just like a teenage fuck,
    In short, our sales could not have been more sickly
If we'd been published first in Volapuk.
    (I'm sorry if this sounds unduly prickly,
But worse than any critic's casual violence
Is when a book's received in chilling silence.)

To date, you see, you've had just seven reviews,
    Too few when you consider how much strife
Your life has caused us both. Though most enthused,
    They said I should have used a sharper knife
When quoting from your verse. I stand accused
    Of being too long-winded in your life
As well as mine! If only I'd condensed it –
That's bollocks. We were always up against it.

You will, I'm sure, be gratified to know
    Our book came out in time for the centenary
Of bloody Eric Bair (see more below).
    His monumental Lives obscured the scenery
So thoroughly that nothing else could grow.
    Like one who takes possession of a deanery
He brought with him the sanctimonious air
Precisely suited to the Age of Blair.

One Blair is more than anyone deserves,
    But two's enough to turn a man to drink;
These last few years we've needed steady nerves
    To see the People's Flag, once proudly pink,
Fade fast to blue, then brown. This gang preserves
    Their power by spinning, lies and double-think,
Requiring us to spy on one another.
This truly is the era of Big Brother.

Perhaps in such an epoch, it's in keeping
  That people now prefer the TV version,
In which some folk are filmed while they are sleeping
  (Their cloistered life approaches the Cistercian).
It's harmless fun for those who think that peeping
  Is nothing but a passable diversion
From living their own lives, but it creates
A world of Peeping Toms and Keyhole Kates.

Biography's, of course, a game for spies;
  Although we like to think we're being objective
Ours is a voyeuristic art that tries
  To let the reading public play detective
With other people's weaknesses and lies
  (This helps put our own failures in perspective);
But look, I really think it would be better
If I explain the purpose of this letter . . .

The Public Records Office down in Kew
  Is opening up old files from MI5,
Including those they kept on Reds like you.
  Although it seems not all your files survive,
They watched you like a monkey in a zoo
  From 1938–55.
Such dedication's certainly impressive
(It makes my own seem rather less obsessive!)

I tried my best to look the other way.
  I thought that I was strong. I'd done my rattle.
What interest could these files possess *per se*?
  Who cares about this kind of tittle-tattle?
But as all former addicts know, each day
  Presents you with another kind of battle.
I thought that I'd just take a little peep –
And here I am back in again chin-deep.

I don't suppose it's such a big surprise
    To know that they were spying through the lock,
But just how large a creepy enterprise
    It took to follow you around the clock,
The regiment of snoopers, sneaks and spies
    Who shadowed you for years, might be a shock.
I half expect to find some British Stasi
Reporting on your movements on the khazi.

Although your pre-war files were so hush-hush
    That somebody ensured they were 'destroyed',
The reason they developed such a crush
    On you is that somebody was annoyed
Because you wrote that song with Alan Bush
    About the hunger of the unemployed.
It would be funny if we weren't, alas,
Still strangled by this loathsome Traitor Class.

There's several hundred entries in your file
    (Including some so secret they're *still* blank).
It's one part Keystone Cops, one part *The Trial*:
    There's stolen letters, statements from your bank,
The contents of your suitcases, your style
    Of dress ('unkempt'!), the pubs in which you drank,
Verbatim transcripts of your private calls,
The friends you met, the pictures on your walls.

They followed you round London day and night,
    Took notes when you addressed a public meeting
(Your précised speeches are most erudite!)
    Their pedantry and zeal would take some beating,
Extending from the trivial to the trite –
    One nark observed, as you were just completing
A five hour pub-crawl, that you had the air
Of one – I kid you not – the worse for wear.

They even had a mole, a friend of sorts,
    A drinking pal with whom you often nattered,
This wretched creature used to send reports
    Direct to Roger Hollis (hope you're flattered)
Informing him of all your private thoughts
    On poetry and art – as if they mattered!
I don't suppose your stoolie ever knew
That Hollis was the Soviet spy – not you!

They put you under 'Special Observation'
    When you joined up and started signal training.
Each month your CO sent them information
    (I think you'd find his letters entertaining)
About the 'Private Swingler situation'.
    By Autumn '43, they were complaining
That they'd lost track of you, demanding bitterly
To know what were you up to out in Italy.

In case the reference isn't understood
    (And there aren't many who will still remember
That eighteen-month campaign of rain and blood),
    Since landing at Salerno in September
You'd pushed the *Werhmacht* back through miles of mud
    To reach the Gustav Line by late December.
While your lot opened up the road to Rome
They opened up new files on you back home.

Along the road from Kirkuk to Trieste
    You thought you knew what you were fighting for,
But as your war-time files make manifest,
    Theirs was a rather different kind of war.
In post-war London (as I'm sure you guessed)
    They exercised their influence to ensure
You lost that staff-job at the BBC.
Such were the costs of keeping Britain free.

We now know Eric Blair was naming names,
    Providing lists of Reds (including you),
An act that every would-be Squealer claims
    Was justified because the lists were true!
Embarrassing, of course, but no-one blames
    A Blair for doing what he has to do
(Or democratic States, when fighting Terror,
For murdering civilians in error).

Like sleepless Argus with his peacock-eyes,
    Or Cerberus, the watch-dog of the Dead,
This hundred-headed Hydra never dies;
    Try cutting off a head and in its stead
More poisonous heads sprout forth, like bigger lies,
    And so the monstrous tongues of falsehood spread,
What Bakhtin might have called a pseudo-glossia,
Until they constitute a dodgy dossier.

Dishonesty is now its own discourse.
    By 'pain-acquired intelligence' they mean
Confessions under torture, which of course
    Then justifies their right to 'intervene'
With what the White House calls 'the greatest force
    For liberty the world has ever seen'.
It's hard to say if this mendacious burble's
More suited to Pinocchio or Goebbels.

Because those flabby liberties of ours
    Were out of shape, they've lately been massaged.
Since the assault on those Manhattan towers
    The secret state's considerably enlarged;
No doubt the State will find that these new powers
    (Six weeks' detention without being charged)
Will come in handy fighting girls in burkas
Or striking low-paid public-sector workers.

The Romans knew how well this trick succeeds.
　The prospect of barbarians at the gate
Convinces the *res publica* it needs
　The sly protection of the wolfish State,
(And what big ears it has!) till someone reads
　The small-print and we realise too late
The enemy invented by New Labour's
The spitting image of our next-door neighbours.

These days it seems our government's at war
　With those whose cause it used to once profess,
Re-branded as the undeserving poor,
　A drain upon the hard-pressed NHS;
The rich can't help themselves for wanting more,
　While those who cannot help themselves get less.
In Britain if you can't afford a peerage
Then you must travel all your life in steerage.

In such an age of salivating snobbery,
　Democracy now wears an Eton boater
And Freedom's code for economic robbery.
　The delicacies offered to the voter
Are either bare-arsed sleaze or bare-faced jobbery.
　Equality's a dream that gets remoter.
When talking of the have-nots and the haves
The working-class is now known as the Chavs.

That's 'Council House and Violent' in the slang
　Of columnists who earn a lot of dosh
By writing Jeremiads which harangue
　All those they think require a decent wash,
Especially if they're in a feral gang
　(Like Downing Street and Violent, but less posh),
Historians of New Labour's wizard struggles
Against the rest of us – that is, the Muggles.

This struggle at the international level
  Is best expressed where Chav becomes *Chavista*,
A movement of the poor that's put the revel
  In *revolución popularista*
Who are at last prepared to kick the devil
  Residing in the White House in the keister.
In short, the revolution in Caracas
Is driving Langley's Latin Bureau crackers.

Fidel's still with us, though he's getting on,
  A symbol of the Cuban Revolution,
Though god knows what will happen when he's gone.
  The USA will make their contribution,
That's fair to say – since 1961
  They've spent a fortune planning retribution;
The Neocons believe in *Cuba libra*
Like cheetahs do in freedom for the zebra.

And so the planet keeps on spinning round,
  Propelled by fear and want and paranoia;
Imperial apologists expound
  A visionary future out of Goya,
And though the Ship of State has run aground
  It's going to be re-launched as a Destroyer.
A small investment this, when you consider
How Freedom's auctioned to the highest bidder.

You'd really think by now we would have learned.
  This global warming's caught us on the hop,
Of course the poor have got their fingers burned,
  But no-one cares, as long as we can shop.
Though everybody's naturally concerned
  When any Big Cat's threatened with the chop,
It's hardly likely that the poor old zebra
Will ever be the public's *cause célèbre*.

Oh sod these bloody zebras and hyenas.
    I need to give this stanza form a break
Before this correspondence comes between us;
    Ottava rima makes my poor brain ache,
Next time I write I ought to try sestinas
    (Which after this should be a piece of cake)
Except, you see, I really don't intend
To write again. This is the end, old friend.

I promise that this really is goodbye,
    You won't be hearing any more from me;
That's it – we're through, finis, decree nisi,
    And honestly, this time I guarantee
I really don't expect you to reply;
    I may be slow, but even I can see
That I must learn to earn my daily bread
Among the Quick and not among the Dead.

Of course there's no point writing to a ghost,
    The correspondence closes when we're dead,
And all we ever leave behind's at most
    The memory of the stupid things we've said,
A bulging file of intercepted post,
    Remaindered like a book that no-one's read,
The failures which in living and in art
We cling to till we know them off by heart.